MONETIZING IDEAS FROM STARTUP TO SUCCESS

I0502647

JACK MCNAUGHTON

CREATING A PROFITABLE BUSINESS

THE ESSENTIAL HANDBOOK FOR ENTREPRENEURS

DEDICATION

For the many friends from Lakeland House Publishing LLP who encouraged me to put into words the years of experience in Startups and fund raising, Thank you.

CONTENTS

PREFACE

Throughout history, stories abound of fabulous riches that a few lucky souls made by coming up with a new and revolutionary idea. Many times, it was like a lottery win, completely random and unexpected.
With new ideas, there are ways to change the odds of winning the lottery of success.
Moreover, it doesn't involve placing our lives into the hands of others.
Instead, it requires a series of dedicated and often passionate steps to be taken towards a defined goal.
If you're ready to pursue an approach that requires work and dedication, then the results will not be a random success story.
Your success will be the direct result of your own experiences and efforts.
Enjoy your journey.

Jack Mcnaughton 2019

1 THE DIAMONDS IN YOUR BACKYARD

"An old priest told an ancient Persian farmer, Ali Hafed, that if he had a handful of diamonds, he could purchase a whole country, and with a mine of diamonds he could place his children upon thrones through the influence of their great wealth.

After Al Hafed heard all about diamonds and how much they were worth, he went to his bed discontented thinking he is a poor man - He said, "I want a mine of diamonds! I want to be immensely rich."

So, he sold the farm and took the money to seek his fortune. He left his family with friends and set-out to seek his fortune. He wandered the world but never found diamonds. He was destitute, lost and depressed. So, he threw himself into the sea to end his suffering.

Later, the same old priest who had told Ali Hafed about diamonds came to visit the new owner of the farm. He saw a flash of light on the table. He rushed over and said, "Here is a diamond - here is a diamond! Has Ali Hafed returned?"

"No, no. Ali Hafed has not returned, and that is not a diamond. That is nothing but a stone. We found it right out there in the garden."

"But I know a diamond when I see it," said the Priest; "That is a diamond! "

It did not look like a diamond. It was in its raw and uncut state. In fact, upon closer inspection, they found that the farm was rich in diamonds. Thus the diamond mines of Golconda were discovered, the most magnificent diamond mines in all the history of humanity."

(Taken from Russel H .Conwell's "Acre of Diamonds" lecture, Temple University.)

It is easy to overlook the skills and life experiences that you accumulate when you are searching for success thru a viable idea. There are many stories of simple meetings and chance happenings creating profitable businesses.

Jim McCann, who grew tired of being a bartender, bought a flower shop for $USD10,000 in 1976. After expanding to 13 shops, he decided to acquire a phone number in 1986 that spelled out "FLOWERS." 1-800-FLOWERS was born and soon became a marketing masterstroke. Adopting this approach for the internet by adding COM, he was able to move into the rapidly developing online shopping explosion. By 2011, his total revenues exceeded $USD680 million annually.

What causes us to ignore the wealth of our own experiences and talent? Why are we blinded to those things around us that others see, and we don't?

Our own inbuilt bias and belief systems can create blind spots. Research has shown that our attitudes inhibit our reasoning. Ideas that challenge our beliefs, regardless of their logical conclusions, are difficult for us to accept. Illogical arguments seem rational if they conform to our current expectations.

Monetizing Ideas is a combination of several skills:

- selecting an idea by recognizing that we filter out many of the opportunities around us, preferring to look at those things that reinforce what we want to believe or that support our agenda and arguments rather than what we can exploit for monetary gain.
- Developing that idea into a viable plan, and
- Implementing that plan.

These are the skills you need as a starting point to find and monetize your diamond ideas.

This book takes you on a journey from the creation of ideas to their exploitation for money. It deals with the often quoted saying that there are a million ideas in the world at any time, but they never get implemented.

George R.R. Martin who is best known for his Novels, *A Song of Ice and Fire* that was adapted to the series *Game of Thrones* commented that *"Ideas are cheap. I have more ideas now than I could ever write up. To my mind, It's the execution that is all-important."* And yes, it is the execution and implementation that brings to life an idea. However, without any ideas, you have nothing to execute.

In this book, a list approach is adopted wherever possible as a means of simplifying the message.

2 LOVE YOUR SWEET SPOT

Overcoming our filters and inbuilt bias is the first step in utilizing numerous methods to aid in idea creation. Many of these methods are published regularly and taught at business schools, standard amongst them being group brainstorming sessions.

We need to battle with our own mental bias and filters as a prelude to utilizing techniques designed to help in idea creation.

We need to move beyond our usual circles and networks. Moreover, be able to listen to competing agendas, ideas and thoughts without automatically discarding those views counter to our own. Such an approach is challenging on many levels, and a slow start is needed to make a change. However, by observing other views, mixing in new networks, reading different newspapers and books, further new information and mental connections can be absorbed. With that new information, you can allow yourself to visualize and daydream.

By meditating or daydreaming you allow the brain to test new connections that were previously blocked. To look at the world and business from different angles using the new thoughts that you have opened up.

Once on this path you can also start to appreciate the new-found confidence and skills you are gaining that causes ideas to form and to grow. Any ideas that you begin to formulate should identify what problems you are addressing, and you need to consider if the concept is novel, useful and viable. Try not to be limited to ideas that seem only significant and vital. Moreover, don't exclude ideas involving issues of trust and cultural change.

One of the many approaches to use in idea formation is the "S.I.T. Method." Various other approaches like Edward de Bono's "lateral thinking" can require a great deal of training. However, Genrich Altshuller worked on a more practical approach to being creative.

His "Systematic Inventive Thinking" (S.I.T.) used a structured approach by taking an existing or new product or idea and then:

- Removed one essential element from any insight or existing part and looked to see what happened (Subtraction);

- Added a similar component or item and checked what resulted (Multiplication);

- Separated the elements into many parts and looked at each piece anew (Division);

- Tried the idea in a new and different way or as a new function (Task Unification); and

- Played with the variables by creating and reducing them (Attribute Dependency).

The purpose of these techniques is an aid in discovering what you can build mentally. The process creates new thoughts and ideas. This "brain training" utilizes your existing skill sets, that is, your very own diamonds that you already have. Because the skills are yours and accessible, you are already in the "sweet spot" ready to exploit that idea.

With new ideas able to enter your thoughts, you can focus on the task of selecting the ideas that you want to turn into your business without them being put aside by your own mental bias. To commence, write down your thoughts and be able to describe them in as much detail as you can.

You must be able to know where the idea(s) lead!

3 THE DROP PIN

To be able to get to a destination, we need to know where we are and where we are going. While such a statement appears self-evident, the adrenaline of a new project can lead to a rush of activity that may be both wasteful and time-consuming and ultimately act to slow down the idea implementation.

Resources needed to develop a new idea are very scarce, and you must nurture them. Moreover, you should ensure these resources are culturally aligned; that is, the choices you make should not offend the cultural norms in your area. By searching out collaborators, or better, co-designers, you can draw upon the support and energy of participants with you on your journey.

You have heard before about successful ideas proven-up on the back of a paper napkin in a bar. The critical point is not the plan itself but the realistic and pragmatic assessment of the marketplace and competition, costs, distribution channels and possible price points and margins for an idea together with an understanding of the forecast demand.

The traditional approach is to create a business plan setting out all elements and variables that can affect a business. However, take care that it is a realistic plan and that it attempts to deal with what is known and addresses the risks of what it could be that is unknown. Many business plans focus on the forecast financial costs, whereas they calculate revenue and sales as a percentage of the market and with arbitrary estimated yearly and compounding growth forecasts. Such approaches fail to weight the real risk factors around those forecast numbers adequately. A realistic assessment of your idea needs a pragmatic approach to evaluating what and even how and when you measure a concept as a success.

The resulting plan is your guide to the reality of the project and should be tested to gauge that your concept can resonate with others in the way that you think.

A business plan is NOT all that useful as a guide to your ability to raise money to help you to market. A study conducted by Babson College found that a business plan was not a prediction of the success in raising investment.

Spend your time wisely and get to understand the key parameters that influence your idea. Test those parameters and a sample of the product before deciding to expend money and time on its development. After you have proven that the project is potentially viable and likely to meet its goals, then you can factor in those steps needed to meet the planned targets.

There are many documented approaches to the creation of a business plan. Also, there are as many tools on offer to assist in drafting a comprehensive plan. In summary, the steps to follow are broken down into:

- researching your market extensively before developing your plan;
- Know what your plan is aiming to achieve. Is it to understand the viability, project rates of return, understand risk and break-even points or to test the validity of your view that the idea is worth undertaking?
- Lay out the business you want people to understand. Its structure, location, licenses, contact points, unique selling points, products, techniques, distribution, capital, debt, assets, opportunities and risks, team, and material contracts;
- How will you market this product and to whom? How big is this market? How will you even enter into the market? What are the pricing structures and why that price?

Business Plans also commence with an Executive Summary. It is very like an Elevator Pitch. Moreover, its purpose is also the same, to entice you into wanting to know more about the idea and business. It is best when you make the Executive Summary direct and easy to read. The Executive is a summary and not the place for detail, rather be clear as to what the idea and business are doing and the problem it is solving. Touch briefly on the market and financial potential and your unique selling point. Finish your Executive Summary with a "call to action" by stating what is needed and by when. Do not leave yourself or your audience wondering what you want and why! An Executive Summary is at most two pages, but you should endeavor to keep it as short as possible and preferably down to one page.

The business plan process commences by proving to yourself that an idea is worth pursuing. It can then be adapted to show collaborators, clients, and investors the merit in the design.

In recent times a new concept suggests that "Start-ups" need to adopt an approach known as being "lean." A business takes its new idea and attempts to create a "product" as quickly and as cheaply as possible. This "Minimum Viable Product" (MVP) is designed to confirm and test if the product will resonate with the market in the way envisaged.

The market testing of the MVP allows for a feedback loop to exist and to identify the need for change, enhancements, exit from the project, redeveloping it, rebranding it and even repositioning the MVP to address the market opportunity better. The intention is that by being in business, you learn quickly how the market will respond to your MVP.

You're well on your way so now you need to do something about it, Implementation!

4 ACT TO WIN

You want to win, and that means turning your idea into an operating business. The process can be a daydream, or it can be decisive. In 1949 Earl Prevette set out that process and pointed to four "laws" that that are needed.

Those four laws are Faith, Repetition, Imagination, and Persistence (FRIP).

It is not enough to verbally explain the problems your business is solving and the opportunities you're offering investors and customers.

Non-verbal communication is the key to developing an interpersonal relationship with others. Effective non-verbal communication leads to the building of trust and the adoption of the belief you have in the idea and now the project.

Such is the power of your faith in the project that it shows through with your actions and emotions. The self-confidence is present in your posture, eye contact, speech strength and various facial expressions amongst many other cues. This Faith in the Business is conveyed to the other party in a non-verbal way and commences to remove any barriers to adopting your beliefs.

The law of repetition is the perfection that can arise from repeating the same process over and over. The expression "practice makes perfect" is a mantra repeated to reinforce the need to keep doing a task and to keep perfecting it with each repetition.

We usually think of such continuous processes for improvements in the manufacturing sector as inspired by W. Edward Deming. He showed that repeated fine adjustments produce better, cheaper and faster output and that any business or plan can improve in this way.

Ideas are visualizations and, in this area, the law of imagination comes to the fore. It is a necessary step to allow the mind to roam, turning the idea over and inside out. Consider the many ways it can be viewed and changed. Can you "think outside the box"? Does it have application in unexpected ways and places?

With the first three laws, you have belief, perfection processes (repetition), and visualization of its application. The final of the Prevette four "laws," Persistence, is often the most difficult. In launching an idea, there will be "potholes" in the road ahead. Without the drive to continue to move the project and design forward, it will become stagnant — the stagnation results in a loss of belief and faith.

Persistence is the driver that aids in your goal attainment by the implementation of your idea into a viable business. However, we are never usually taught how to accomplish our goals.

Implementation is where most new ideas fail. We understand the need for faith, repetition, imagination, and persistence. It is in the implementation phase that will test your ability to apply those four "laws." You will find a steep learning curve during the implementation phase, discovering those things you did not think about and those things you did not know.

As you implement your ideas, develop "feedback loops" within your business that will assist you in deciding what is working and what needs improving. Without this feedback, you cannot assess if your ideas are working out as you intended. Developing any new idea means you are an innovator and a change agent. Recognize that change requires courage in implementing that original idea.

You will be confronting many obstacles and barriers, including your fears, distractions, belittlement by others, being taken advantage of by collaborators and a world filled with competitors happy to use your ideas for their benefit.

In 1999 Peter Golwitzer researched a concept he called "implementation intentions." What he found was that your goals are more likely to be achieved when you can specifically identify behaviours you want to happen in response to future events. He was very precise with his concept and, it was much more than an "I want" desire. It drilled down to possible situations where **if** a specific situation arises **then** I will respond in this way.

The concept is about planning the "when, where and how" we act so the results we are striving to achieve, our intentions, will progress despite the many roadblocks that confront the implementation of an idea. The concept calls this "planning prompts."

Todd Rogers et al. (2015) suggests that the following situations in which the use of planning prompts are useful:

- "When strong intentions already exist,
- When these intentions are intrinsically motivated,
- When at least some obstacles exist,
- When no current plan exists,

- When the risk of forgetting to act is high,
- When the timeline for action is finite,
- When planning will induce people to consider specific barriers to activity,
- When there is a future time for work,
- When people can think correctly about implementation details,
- When there are opportunities to share plans publicly,
- When planning for single rather than multiple goals, and
- When there is a low likelihood that unanticipated moments for action will arise".

The Great Britain Olympic goal medal 8's rowing team adopted this approach as part of their Olympics preparation. The team knew that to win a GOLD medal at the Olympics, and they had to improve by several seconds over their current personal best times. The group decided to adopt the Implementation Intention Theory to help them achieve their goal.

In their program, they prepared "planning prompts" that asked a series of "if-then" style questions. Such as "I want to party and drink beer tonight." The prompt leads to an answer that says, "**If** I do that, **then** I will lose time when rowing." This prompt lead to the action they should take to achieve their goal. "Is that desirable? If not, then it should be rejected."

They prepared a range of these "if-then" scenarios and agreed on the action to take when the situation arose.

The methodology needed to adopt the concept of "implementation intention" is to recognize that you need to decide beforehand, a "pre-decision," to follow a desirable path that supports the implementation of your stated goal. Implementation intention planning is not a business plan. It is an action plan to avoid obstacles that impede you reaching your goals.

Peter Gollwitzer's studies showed that this simple approach **doubled** the chance of getting to your goal.

Based on their research, Wieber and Gollwitzer also identified several results that arise from adopting their theory. Dr. Timothy A. Pychyl summarised their research in 2010:

- You're more likely to get started when you put the stimulus for action into your environment;
- Your Implementation Intentions have measurable effects that are greater than being only motivated to succeed. They help to keep you on course to your goal;
- You can facilitate the disengagement that can be problematic in your goal pursuit by assisting you to disengage from ineffective strategies. That is, if you are unsure, uncertain or unclear you can become frozen and unable to take the actions needed to implement your plans. By having a Plan B available, you can switch tracks and

unfreeze your efforts, provided you have alternate plans available as part of your pre-decision planning prompts;

- You can prevent "burn-out" of your willpower (self-regulation depletion). Studies have confirmed that when you control your emotions, you affect your willpower into the future. The studies showed that by using the implementation intentions approach and by pre-deciding "if (this situation arises) - then (I can take that action towards achieving my goal)," that you strengthened your willpower.

There have now been over 100 studies verifying that adopting these simple implementation intention strategies work as stated. A 1-2-3 steps summary of these strategies are:

1. Select your goal. The stronger your intentions, the more likely it will work;
2. Plan and create prompts about how you will achieve your goal while attempting to think of the ways it could be blocked or prevented;
3. Construct the "if-then" plans around your prompts and the likely blockages, using the "if (this situation arises) - then (I can take that action towards achieving my goal)."

An example of what a new project "if-then" pre-decision structure might include:

- **If** I need to get a document finished, **then** I will move to a quiet room to avoid the distractions (as I get easily distracted);
- **If** I can't get the decision by Monday, **then** I need to have an alternative Plan B in place;
- **If** I can't find a contact for venture capital company to help my project, **then** I will ask my mentor to locate one;
- **If** I have a busy day ahead, **then** I will prioritize my work and remove all unnecessary actions and distractions.

Implementation intention planning is a straightforward yet proven goal attainment tool. Somewhat oddly, the effect of thinking about the goals and blockages results in more motivation and an improved chance of achieving the goal because you have become mentally attuned to overcoming blockages (Gabriele Oettingen's demonstrated concept of Mental Contrasting).

You are probably also working with others in teams and groups. The thinking and behaviours prevalent amongst all groups when attempting to implement a goal are often significantly impacted by the "project prevention team." You can identify them as the ones who cause the most delays and hinder progress while telling you they want to project to proceed.

Statements such as "let's meet next week to discuss!" should be a red flag to you. They need to be deemed an obstacle or blockage to achieving your goal. When you see this behaviour, you know it is the time to introduce the appropriate planning prompts using the "if-then" implementation strategy to deal with the obstacles created by the group members. Don't underestimate the effect of these group members. They can delay your project to the point of collapse and are easily one of the biggest hurdles you need to battle. The option to isolate or remove them needs to be part of your plan.

The action to get a project started and not be side-tracked requires you and your team to recognize that there is a reluctance to commence. How often have you heard about non-priority matters stopping the critic work from starting?

- I need a desk, office, paperclips, business cards, letterhead before I can get started on the project;
- I will begin tomorrow, and I need to visit my friends today;
- I need to undertake another course to appreciate what I need to do; and
- I need to do more research.

These obstacles also need to be identified together with the team members and planned around so the group can act in unison to pre-decide what actions they take when obstacles appear.

Finally, it would be best if you also recognized the reality that one of the blockages may be that the plan will never work or needs a dramatic overhaul. So the most important of all your programs is knowing when to call it quits on a project. Determine benchmarks in your implementation intentions to include "breakpoints." Stick to them unless it is clear there have been material changes.

Carrying out such programs as S.I.T. and Implementation Intentions planning is not easy. It would be best if you continually worked at your plan. Remember, thousands of ideas never get implemented. If you want to avoid your projects adding to the pile of discarded great ideas that never see the light of day, then decisive action will be needed.

5 MY DIY TOOLBOX

Have you heard that the idea cannot proceed because there is no cash for the business? However, "Where there is a will, there is a way!".

Any individual who has started a business on a shoestring knows how to bootstrap or stretch the cash flow - both in monetary terms and something else usually referred to as scavenging - to the extent they can. However, bootstrapping isn't constrained to start-ups. It's a legitimate path for entrepreneurs to use regardless of where you are in the business cycle.

In 2018 early stage start-ups received $28 billion from investors with the median size investment of $7 million. However, only one in five thousand companies will get venture capital, and almost one-third of all small businesses commenced with less than $5,000.

Bootstrapping implies that less cash is needed to get the job done! Bootstrapping is a conservative approach to allow a business to operate and complete the processes that are part of the implementation plan.

Specific approaches vary by country and are dependent upon local conditions. Listed here are a few of those approaches to consider, but they are by no means all those involved in bootstrapping a business.

The "Creditor's Bank" is one approach to improve cash flow. Delaying paying an invoice for purchases for 90 days, without interest, certainly aids in improving the outflow of cash. However, you will always need to know that, as a "start-up," financial credit will be difficult and being a "slow payer" will affect future relationships with credit providers. Nevertheless, some organizations when approached, and who are comfortable with your trustworthiness and business plan, may grant extended trade terms. Try this approach, and you may be surprised at the result.

One example was a Buyer group that had identified a market for a vitamin that appealed to their market. However, they realized they could not afford to buy the inventory needed to win a significant contract as it called for reliable suppliers with a minimum inventory holding and 90-day credit terms. They approached their vitamin manufacturer and explained that they had the potential for a sizeable recurring order, but they were not able to take on that opportunity as they had insufficient inventory and did not have the working capital available to finance improved inventory levels with extended trade terms.

The manufacturer assessed that it would be in his interest to extend credit to 180 days from the present COD - at a slightly higher purchase price. The manufacturer calculated he would benefit from ongoing sales, improved factory productivity, enhanced volume discounts and entry into a market area previously unavailable. With this cash flow and inventory support, the Buyer rapidly expanded his market share with only a small drop in margins but a much-improved net profit and cash flow.

Continually being reliant on extended trade credit terms from a single creditor is not always the safest of options. Your business may turn out to be over-reliant on those providers. Accordingly, the company may never again have access to other aggressive providers who offer lower costs, a unique product, and better services.

Further, early-payment discounts can equate to significant improvements in profit margin. This improved margin can be the difference in your business gaining market share and being profitable.

The sale of your invoices and purchase orders (factoring), is another way to improve cash flow and free up money for business growth and survival. There are many types of factoring, but the common element is the sale of the invoice or purchase order for immediate cash payment with an amount held back until the debtor finally pays the invoice.

The calculation of any benefit in factoring depends on the time value of money and the cash flow impact plus any offsetting advantages like getting purchase discounts or improving sales by being able to buy inventory. Any decision to use a cash flow enhancement approach like factoring is a case of aligning your choice with the goals and plans of your business.

There are other financing methods for inventory, car floor-plans, bank working capital overdrafts, and asset security leasing and renting that can act to fund the cash requirements of the business. However, they often come with the demand for guarantees and security charges over personal and business assets. You must carefully consider the decision to pledge assets to obtain funding. The survival rate of new small businesses, with an unproven idea, is generally meagre and you need to recognize this higher risk in your wealth and risk-based decision making.

Expenses and fixed assets purchases have a dramatic effect on the cash flow of your business. Also, in the early stages alternatives such as working from home, co-working spaces, borrowed and loaned premises, cars, and other assets reduce the cash needed as well as the guarantees pledged.

Remember any financing is a loan and must be secured and repaid. Moreover, the repayment of loans and other fixed commitments place your cash flow under "stress" with their servicing obligations leaving the venture at a higher risk of failure. Great care should be exercised to keep fixed costs at the lowest possible level. They should never reach the stage where they exceed a small percentage of the recurring reliable and stable cash flow.

Assessing the risk of failure and the resulting consequences must form part of all your debt-based funding considerations. Never hope for the best, instead plan and understand the implications of failure using the "if-then" approach.

Renting and outsourcing is another approach to reduce the financing of high-ticket items like machinery, vehicles, furniture, PCs and even staff and sales representatives. Renting and outsourcing means you pay for what you use, as opposed to paying the entire buy cost up front or by debt with recurring commitments. When you're beginning, it may bode well to search around and get the best combination of transactional overhead arrangements possible. This approach makes the overheads a variable cost based upon and preferably linked to sales completed, and cash received. For instance, you could outsource transactions based upon commission only, use offices on a pay as you go basis and locate "free" services that only charge as you scale-up.

Bootstrap financing truly starts and finishes with your regard for the careful management of your money and assets. Know about what you spend and minimize your overhead. Make trading for products and services your preferred system when it is proper to do so. If possible, use the "barter" concept rather than cash.

There are many famous examples of companies that bootstrapped their ideas during the implementation and growth stages. The GoPro founder used his savings and a small loan from his mother in 2002 to grow his business until 2012 when the Taiwanese manufacturer, Foxconn, invested $USD200 million. In 2014 GoPro went public with a $2.96 Billion company valuation.

Craigslist started as an email service in 1995. The Craigslist founder operated it mainly as a small project. In 2004 eBay paid $32 million for 28% of Craigslist because it was attracting millions of page views monthly. By 2016 Craigslist gross revenues exceeded $690 million.

GitHub cost its owners a few thousand dollars to establish in 2008. They operated it from their local coffee shops and homes. By 2012 they had raised $100 million and by 2015 GitHub was valued at $2 billion.

These stories are inspirational and show that the founders did not take on excessive debt risk early in the start-up phase. Monitor and control debt and any security pledged. Plan to establish strong sales before venturing too far into cash outflows that require an increase in your business survival risk.

The risk to your financial security that comes with business decisions must be considered carefully and with expert advice. Cash flow pressures and other business worries do affect your abilities to operate a successful business by creating anxiety. It is best if you acknowledge that when you are controlling your fears attaching to the risks from the business; offering guarantees, cash flow pressures and the like, you trigger the "self-regulation depletion" effect causing a burn-out in your will-power thereby affecting your future decision-making abilities.

6 BUCKLE UP

Now that you are operating, you have many aspects of the business to consider. Care should be taken not to concentrate your efforts on areas that are not important or critical to the business's profitability and progression. Your Implementation Intention planning process should now be used to reach your next goal.

It is the case that many entrepreneurs are side-tracked into many other areas of a business that often are time-consuming "black holes." Completing the Implementation Intention plan must be the priority. Obstacles such as non-essential tasks must be outsourced or left. Dealing with the urgent need to replace the photocopier paper rather than making a sales call is only one example of a misallocation of time. They are obstacles to reaching your goal.

This same focus on priorities must be the guiding rule throughout the business.

You will need to establish clear rules for executing and observing the operation of your plan with the implementation team, including:

- Protecting your IP from the outset;
- Ensuring that all family and staff recognize the business priorities. In an active business, this is critical. It amounts to extending the Implementation Intention plans to incorporate your entire group;
- Planning to ensure every individual knows their jobs and employment obligations;
- Building up clear guidelines in all the main areas of the business;
- Deciding how you will encourage "feedback loops" that are designed to challenge all aspects of the business amongst staff and associated outsiders. It will lead to a state of continuous improvement of the business processes;
- Preparing to continually test the assumptions underlying your

business plan and control costs. It means incorporating the "if-then" planning to link in with all the aspects critical to reaching the goal;

- Developing a plan to monitor and control all significant elements in the plan such as staff performance, sales, profits, expenses, productivity, lead times, cash flows, debt requirements, and business risks. Know what "if-then" pre-decisions are required should this process identify the missed targets and KPIs;

- Searching out complaints and criticism of yourself and the business. Then acting on improving those aspects. Don't ignore blogs and feedback like Trip Advisor. A tarnished brand is an incredible obstacle to your business;

- Another obstacle to your brand is a failure to supply product or services promptly and within the expectations of your customers. Look for possible supply bottleneck points. Then plan for the "if-then" and how it can be corrected;

- Establishing how to benchmark your performance against your plan and others continually;

- Determining how you will promptly deal with problems and risks; and

- Seeking out a mentor, new networks and data on trends likely to affect your business.

7 IT'S MINE! NO! IT'S MINE!

In the planning process, you need to take account of the assets that you have created and identify if there is a risk that failure, for any reason, that may impact on the ownership of the IP. IP protection is a process that attempts to protect the underlying asset created by your idea.

You cannot monetize an idea without your IP being correctly secured. Remember that you may not be all that original in your thinking. Your "idea" may already have been discovered and is already out there in the market. Understanding your IP position from the outset is vital. It is far too late to consider IP protection after you have started and expended money.

There are different areas to consider with IP Protection. When developing your idea take care so that:

- If you're brainstorming with colleagues, you are developing this IP as a group. Deal with IP ownership from the very start. You can use a "founders' agreement," and when you launch your Company you should have those rights assigned to your start-up business;
- If you're creating your idea on someone else's time and using someone else's resources, STOP! Your employers may have "invention assignment agreements" or can claim an interest in the concept;
- You consider the style of structure to use for your business, its benefits and the type of IP rights transfer applicable?
- The nature of the IP Protection, noting that it is also dependent on several legal factors and costs;
- Patents, which are the most robust protection, but are your ideas qualified for a Patent? If your design has a useful purpose and is new or novel, the idea is eligible for patent protection, provided there is not an earlier filing of this idea. Patent filings (and therefore future patent protection) are on a "first come first served basis," so get in

early and first;

- Your idea may already be covered by general Copyright law that covers images, art, text, stories including computer code;
- You trademark particular words, names and logos; and
- You consider patents in other countries.

8 MONEY PLEASE

It is not enough to be able to protect your IP and to finance your business via debt and scavenging. Often you need to be able to sell the business to investors as well as the products your offering to customers. Your ability to communicate becomes pivotal in the next step.

You will recognize those occasions from your own experience when you've asked someone, "what do you do?". How did you feel when they were either slow, unclear and even unsure how to answer this simple question?

Being able to effectively and quickly lay out the reason you have a great business or idea is the hallmark of a successful entrepreneur. The answer to this question means you are competing to gain the focus of a potential investor or customer in a short time frame.

The purpose of your quick response often referred to as an "elevator pitch," is never to close the deal. Instead, it is to engage that person to start to take an interest in what you are doing. You will not gain the answer you want from anyone without them wanting to understand more about your idea.

The basics of any elevator pitch are:
- Keep it simple;
- Create curiosity;
- Have a specific "call-to-action";
- Leave open your story for further questions;
- Be compelling and engaging;
- Pitch to the person you're talking to, that is, understand your audience;
- Always focus on the most attractive aspect of your business;
- Explain the problem you have identified; and

- Summarise the solution that your idea is solving.

Later, in the follow-up phase, you will be able to expand on the elevator pitch with a highly focused pitch deck. The pitch deck presentation is for a targeted audience, and with the presentation pitch deck, you will focus on specific investors, clients or staff. The pitch deck is not a business plan. The Business Plan is typically only discussed much later as part of a due diligence process and as part of an investment or credit analysis.

The pitch deck is designed to cover the business in more detail than an elevator pitch but is usually given as part of a presentation and limited to about 10 to 15 PowerPoint slides.

These slides cover the essential elements of:

- What problem are you solving?
- How will you solve it?
- Who is in the Team and how are they the ones to solve the problem?
- Is anyone else out there doing a similar thing?
- What do you need to make it happen?
- What can go wrong (risks)?
- What will everyone make out of solving the problem?
- Is there an exit plan?

What you need to understand is that with any presentation either as an elevator pitch or as an investor/business pitch deck, you are selling yourself as well as your business. The confidence and follow through discussed in the Prevette four "laws" built around Faith, Repetition, Imagination, and Persistence are to be applied when selling the implementation stage of your business idea.

Selling is an important skill to learn. The techniques taught to salespeople apply equally here. In dealing with the business in your elevator pitch and pitch decks, it is worth noting that you should:

- Search for something more profound for the investor that gives them total self-satisfaction. The investor is your audience and your customer. It is their needs and wants that are being satisfied, not yours;
- It is worth repeating this lack of focus on the audience often as it is the biggest failing in most presentations. The focus must be on your target audience, and this is pre-eminent. Place yourself in their shoes to understand their needs rather than your needs;
- In sales training manuals by "Wilson Learning" they teach that in the sale process, there are four hindrances to winning over a customer:

a) No **Trust** (you are not believable),

b) No **Need** (I don't need this),

c) No **Help** (This doesn't help me) and

d) No **Hurry** (I can decide on this sometime in the future).

Focusing on who is your audience is the primary objective in preparing for a sale or presentation. The biggest pitfall in any potential sale process is to change your focus away from your audience and start to use your needs as the driving force. For example, "I need the money this week to pay the rent." That is not an argument that would assist any investor/customer in understanding why he should invest or buy?

Equally, when you are presenting to investors and clients using any presentation material, for example, PowerPoint slides, you need to remember some simple key elements applicable to your target audience:

- Have you explained to your audience the point of the presentation? It seems a simple thing, but have you ever been to events where the presenter starts but fails to provide an introduction or preamble? By launching straight into your story, you are not engaging with your audience or are you preparing them for your message;

- Try to appeal to the most substantial part of your audience. Do not consider that you are only presenting to a single knowledgeable person but ensure your pitch reaches most of the audience;

- Utilize pictures to convey your message. Try for attention-grabbing images, animations, and variety. Entertaining the customer will help maintain audience attention. The presentation is not a script. Large and bold fonts, simple slides with plenty of white space makes your message stand out. Your audience is not there to read, but they are there to understand the idea and to assess you;

- Ensure your presentation is not crowded. Make the text very large and simple. The more information squeezed onto a slide, the less likely it will be taken in and understood by them. You are trying to convey a message. So, you need to help your audience get it quickly;

- Stay on your storyline. Your presentation is a story and starts like all stories with an introduction, laying out the scene and traveling through to a climax and ending. By following this approach, you carry your audience along, hopefully, just like they're reading an exciting book;

- Ensure you have a consistent formatting structure and font style to maintain the feeling that there is a coherent storyline.

"People judge a book by its cover." So, your appearance does matter because it is true that "first impressions" count. If you fail to make an appropriate first impression, you will struggle to be accepted.

The four hindrances to a "sale" commence with Trust. Your appearance is a factor in gaining trustworthiness. How can you be believable and want people to believe in your idea if you appear not to take time to care about your image? Following classic dress codes can seem to smack of conformity.

However, the sale is "not about you." It is about engaging the needs, emotions, and desires of the audience. Looking smart or looking shabby can be carried off as a matter of style but unless you are capable in this area, play it safe and adopt the uniform expected by the audience.

Your audience will quickly detect the body language you utilize. If you are disorganized, speak uncomfortably, are unclear or off subject, use excessive movements and lousy speech, they will all contribute to the message your conveying. Take care to recognize in yourself the effects such as body language has on you when you see it in the performance of others.

Undertaking a speech and sales course can assist you in mastering and appreciating the motivations and emotions that attach to the "selling" process and at the very least, read about selling methods. Attempt to understand what it is that makes your business and your idea attractive to someone else. That's the first step in ensuring you are approaching your audience correctly.

There are some simple yet extremely effective sales methods that you can learn to use quickly. Research has found that the use of sales techniques such as "mimicry" and "mirroring" greatly enhance your chance of receiving a positive response from your target audience. You must beware that these techniques can also backfire. Mimicry can have both a positive or negative impact.

By and large, mimicry leaves individuals with constructive and positive sentiments about you (Andersen, 1998) and can lead to the view that you are influential (Balinson and Yee, 2005). There is a caveat that, in certain circumstances, it can have the reverse effect (Lui, et al., 2011) and in some environments can be taken as disregarding community norms of behaviour.

You must know your audience and understand what they want. The proposals you put forward must meet those expectations. You must gain their trust and create a feeling of urgency for a decision. You can enhance these effects by adopting proven sales techniques when used correctly.

Not all ideas need to be in the category of essential to be saleable to your audience. In 1975 when the USA was in the middle of oil shortages, and extensive lines were at the petrol pumps Gary Dahl invented the "Pet Rock." His Pet Rock was just that, a rock. His marketing approach was to ignore the fact it was just a rock and package it in such a way that it replicated a living pet which came with care manuals. Moreover, he sold it for $USD4.00 per stone.

9 HELP

There are a variety of additional help programs such as incubators, accelerators, government grants, pre-seed and seed-stage venture funds, corporate venture funds, gifts, cash offers, angel investors and unique bank debt offerings. Look at trying both the pre-purchase and equity crowdfunding approach after you have proven your MVP works

Each of these programs has its strengths and failings. The method that is most often overlooked and may be the fastest way to capitalize on an idea is to find a mentor.

"If you ask any successful businessperson, they will always have had a great mentor at some point along the road. If you want success, then it takes hard work, hard work, and more hard work. However, it also takes a little help along the way. If you are determined and enthusiastic, then people will support you."

Sir Richard Branson

In life, we need some direction, somebody to check in with and seek a realistic opinion on our ideas, somebody who can inspire and debate us. This kind of relationship can bring enormous advantages to both parties. Here are eight key reasons why we all can use a mentor at some stage in our business life:

a) Generally, the mentors offer their time for free and are non-judgmental. There are mentorship arrangers and fee-based mentoring businesses;

b) It would help if you located someone with a broad scope of aptitudes – from how to implement ideas, to showcase items, manage clients, brand building, investor approaches and so on.

c) You can bounce thoughts off them, and they can help you settle on essential choices. For instance, entrepreneurs need to develop ideas quickly which could prompt cash and other issues. The mentor relationship will not guarantee that you don't make errors, but it will be more likely to reduce the mistakes and severity.

d) Sometimes we all need a gentle push.

e) To challenge you that you're on the right path.

f) Your Mentor is probably going to have a vast network. This network is invaluable, having taken many years to accumulate. It can be an essential advantage for you, particularly at the beginning of your business. These associations, for the most part, incorporate investors, providers, wholesalers, and perhaps engages with those involved in promoting and publicizing services and products.

g) It allows you the ability to transition away from aggressive Venture Capital to bootstrapping networks.

The advantages of mentorship are not restricted merely to business enterprises. Research in different fields demonstrates that great mentors will, in general, improve the execution of their protege's plans. Having a great mentor can materially aid in getting your idea to market and your business plan implemented.

The legendary founder of Apple, Steve Jobs, made use of a mentor, Mike Markkula. Jobs wrote in his biography "Mike took me under his wing. His values were much aligned with mine. He emphasized that you should never start a company to get rich. Your goal should be making something you believe in and making a company that will last."

Steve Wozniak, Jobs' partner in the foundation and success of Apple, was quoted as saying that Markkula "was the one man and one person who made Apple a successful company."

Facebook's Zuckerberg relied upon input from Steve Jobs. Google's Page and Brin found Eric Schmidt whom they realized had a vision and a culture like their view. There is no easy answer. Google's Page and Brin searched for over a year and alienated over 50 senior and respected potential mentors before they connected with Schmidt.

It is essential to recognize that:

- Mentoring is not about you;
- A mentor is someone you need to find, and they don't usually search for you;
- Mentoring is never a one-way street. You must be a participant when working with the mentor;
- There are a time and place to seek out a mentor.

There is an extensive array of material on each of the funding options available today. Moreover, by having an experienced mentor in place, you are better positioned to decide if any or all these options are a fit for you. Each option has a range of pros and cons that will change depending on your MVP, location and structure. You need to consider patent and IP rights, local restrictions on your offering and local laws and taxes. These considerations are where your mentor can be invaluable. However, they are not superhuman.

10 **POTHOLES**

An analysis of why start-ups fail has identified that the leading causes of the failure are in the areas of access to money and poor cash flow, weak demand, and poor management. CBI Insights polled start-ups to identify the prime reasons for failures. The results (totalling more than 100%) represent the multiple reasons for failure in the respondent pool of 101 start-ups:

- **42%** failed because there was no market.
- **29%** failed because they ran out of money.
- **23%** failed because they didn't have the right team.
- **19%** failed due to competitors.
- **18%** failed because of pricing and cost issues.
- **17%** failed because of an inferior product offering.
- **17%** failed because they lacked a business model.
- **14%** failed because of poor marketing.
- **14%** failed because they ignored their customers.

These start-up failures were over several years. The USA Bureau of Labor Statistics' Business Employment Dynamics reported (2017) statistics of business survival rates across all business categories. They identified that 20% of USA small businesses fail in year one. By year five, 50% had failed. Specifically, these small businesses had employees, and the survival rates were:

- **79.8%** of companies who have employees survive the first 12 months;
- **69.2%** of companies who have employees survive two years;
- **50.2%** of companies who have employees survive five years;
- **33%** of companies who have employees survive ten years;

You need to include in your "if-then" planning the appropriate plans for business and idea failure. Failure can, and statistically probably will happen to you.

Walt Disney was fired by a newspaper that considered he had no ideas or imagination. He then went on to establish Disneyland now valued more than $35 billion. Henry Ford failed twice in creating car manufacturing businesses, but he was third time lucky with the Ford Motor Company, now worth over $188 billion.

11 **LIFE BALANCE**

The thrill and challenges associated with bringing your idea to life can take a toll on many aspects of your life. You need to apply your newly found skill in using the implementation intention planning prompts and develop actions to create a balanced relationship while implementing your idea. Are you always working on your plan? If so, it may be that you are risking more than failure in monetizing your idea.

Original and fresh thinking can be improved if you are enjoying a balanced life. A balanced life is more than a lifestyle issue as it is critical to your success in monetizing the idea. Moreover, wellbeing is not limited to your physical health.

Commence getting your private "time," family and work into balance by managing your time. Your private "self-time" needs to include exercise, time out with friends, travel and "smelling the roses." There is ample material available on life-work balance. Remember the concept of "burn-out" that affects your future ability to maintain your will power. Your will power is vital to being able to carry on with your ideas and business. It needs protecting.

By allowing your emotions and anxiety to have a release you are aiding in preventing "self -regulation burn-out."

Adopting the "if-then" approach to assist in recognizing difficulties in your life caused by excessive and ongoing control of emotions will help you to avoid significant obstacles to monetizing your idea.

12 HOW DO YOU EAT AN ELEPHANT?

It is best eaten one mouthful at a time. So, it is with getting started.

This book lays out a generic pathway to take into consideration. However, the first steps come from you.

It is understandable that projecting forward and looking at all the matters to be dealt with when visualizing the implementation of an idea can be enough to cause you to freeze up. However, by allocating a small and dedicated short period each day to the most critical items to be dealt with, there can be movement.

Dealing with the hard tasks first works but only if you have them broken into small pieces. Don't overstuff your daily task list. Any wins in finishing even a small job will create a mental and physical success that serves to reinforce acceptable behavior. Success leads to a desire for more success.

The industry of gamification requires you to have a reward, usually a win, to keep you involved and to grow your interest. It's a proven system that you can utilize by having small gains of your own. It works for you and will work for your teams.

Your ultimate prize is also essential. Set achievable goals that can be reached and are realistic. Also, add clear and measurable benchmarks to those goals with a time-limit that is achievable. Ensure you celebrate success when you obtain your goal and reward yourself and your team. Involve your family and friends so they can appreciate the progress you're making and can support your efforts.

These celebrations serve to reinforce mental and physical behaviors that are needed to monetize your ideas.

Good luck with your ideas.

The website www.monetizingideas.tips has additional material and news and a way to make contact and tell your story.

ABOUT THE AUTHOR

Jack Mcnaughton has a Master's in Change, Management, and Leadership from York St. John University in England. He has been responsible for the listing of over 20 companies on exchanges in Europe, North America and Australia with a combined market capitalization above $1.5 billion. He has also been involved with dozens of start-ups and has overseen the raising of more than $100 million in funding for these start-ups. He has created and managed a global network specializing in business creation. He has taught at the MBA level as an Assistant Professor in the Entrepreneurship stream. He is now consulting to several new start-ups and acts as a mentor to several entrepreneurs.

www.ingramcontent.com/pod-product-compliance
Lightning Source LLC
Chambersburg PA
CBHW030738180526
45157CB00008BA/3220